DON'T ASK HOW
BELIEVE IN MIRACLES

GEETA RANGA

BLUEROSE PUBLISHERS
India | U.K.

Copyright © Geeta Ranga 2024

All rights reserved by author. No part of this publication may be reproduced, stored in a retrieval system or transmitted in any form or by any means, electronic, mechanical, photocopying, recording or otherwise, without the prior permission of the author. Although every precaution has been taken to verify the accuracy of the information contained herein, the publisher assumes no responsibility for any errors or omissions. No liability is assumed for damages that may result from the use of information contained within.

BlueRose Publishers takes no responsibility for any damages, losses, or liabilities that may arise from the use or misuse of the information, products, or services provided in this publication.

For permissions requests or inquiries regarding this publication,
please contact:

BLUEROSE PUBLISHERS
www.BlueRoseONE.com
info@bluerosepublishers.com
+91 8882 898 898
+4407342408967

ISBN: 978-93-6452-130-7

First Edition: September 2024

"Look at the Sky. We are not alone . The whole universe is friendly to us and conspires only to give the best to those who dream and work."

- A. P. J. Abdul Kalam

This book is dedicated to my daughters Himika and Diksha , my greatest hope for a brighter future. Whose love and laughter fill my life with joy.

About the Author

Hello readers, Thank you for taking the time to learn a little about me.

From the beginning of my career, I have always believed in the power of continuous growth and transformation. With a B.Sc. and a Postgraduate diploma in Garment Manufacturing Technology from NIFT (National Institute of Fashion Technology), I started my journey in 1999 as a Merchandiser in a garment export house. But my true passion led me to academics, where I began teaching as a Fashion Design Faculty member in 2006. This eventually inspired me to found Maxx Academy in 2009, where I serve as Director.

In 2021, I expanded my expertise by becoming a Certified Transformation Coach, Mind Power Trainer, and Certified Meditation Teacher, focusing on stress management and emotional wellness. My journey has shown me firsthand how powerful the mind is in shaping our reality. The universe responds to our thoughts and beliefs—it's as simple as asking, believing, and receiving, without worrying about how it will happen.

Our subconscious mind holds immense potential, capable of turning our deepest desires into reality. This book is a collection of my personal stories, each highlighting the transformative power of the mind. I hope these experiences inspire you to believe in the universe and unlock the incredible capabilities within your own mind.

Contents

The Untold Tales

1. From Dream to Desk
2. From Despair to Miracle
3. Wish Upon a Board
4. From Desperation to Triumph
5. From Wish to Reality
6. Mastering Manifestation
7. A Young Dreamer
8. The Universe's Canvas
9. Finding Purpose beyond Success
10. Dream, Believe, Achieve

The Secrets to How

1. Clarity
2. Focus
3. Raising Vibrations
4. Taking Action
5. Visualization
6. Surrender
7. Believe in Divine Timing
8. Affirmations
9. Celebrate your Success
10. Pursuing your Passion

"All the powers in the Universe are already ours. It is we who have put our hands before our eyes and cry that it is dark."

- Swami Vivekananda

From Dream to Desk

1

During my post-graduation, I read some books on subconscious mind so I usually tried to understand and apply whatever I could learn from those books. It was during my third semester, and I was getting ready for campus interviews.

What I wanted most was to work in a beautiful, luxurious office. The salary didn't matter much to me. My main wish was for the office to have amazing infrastructure and interiors, so stunning that I would look forward to going there every day.

White has always been my favorite colour, so I imagined my office with white interiors. I pictured everything in white. In my mind, the office reception was grand, with exquisite decor. I would imagine myself walking into the reception, feeling a surge of happiness and thinking, "Wow, Geeta, what a wonderful place to work." The receptionist would greet me with a big smile, full of enthusiasm. Then, I would walk to my cabin, open the door, and see a beautiful room with white interiors. I imagined myself working hard, and when I got tired, I would rest my head on the back of my chair and look at the calm sea in front of me. The calmness of the sea always made me feel at peace. This was my daydream every single day. I would visualize it and feel so happy, even though it was just a dream.

Finally, the day of the campus interview arrived. It was an exciting yet nerve-wracking time. I had been waiting for this day for so long. I felt a mix of excitement and anxiety as I walked into the interview room. There, I saw a panel of five managers waiting to interview me. They smiled and asked me to sit down.

The interview began, and everyone asked me questions. I answered them confidently, feeling a sense of relief with each response. The managers seemed pleased with my answers. After what felt like an eternity, they finally selected me. They called me to their office next day, and I was thrilled beyond words.

The office was at Nariman Point in Mumbai. I was so excited to see my office before joining. When I reached the 14th floor, I stepped into the reception and was amazed. It looked fantastic. The receptionist greeted me with a big smile, just like I had imagined. The director then took me on a tour of the office. The interior was mostly brown, and I felt a bit disappointed because I had wanted everything to be white.

But then, the director said, "Let me show you your cabin." I was thrilled to hear that I would have my own space. As we entered the cabin, my mouth dropped open in surprise. Everything inside was white! The table, chair, walls, bookshelf, desktop computer, landline phone, and even the blinds on the windows—all white. I couldn't believe it. It was as if someone had seen into my mind and brought them to life. The picture I had in my mind was right there in front of me, but this time it wasn't a dream.

The director asked me to sit in the chair. As I leaned back, he opened the blinds, and there it was—the sea, calm and vast, just as I had imagined. I was speechless. I stared at the sea and thought, "How could anyone know this? How did this all come true?"

The sea was quiet, but I felt as though it whispered to me, "Don't ask me how."

So, I believe the Universe is always watching, listening, and observing us. We just need to believe in the Universe, give it positive signs, and do all the hard work. The Universe will give us the results of our choice.

" You have to dream before your dreams can come true."

- A. P. J. Abdul Kalam

From Despair to Miracle

2

In 2009, I embarked on a journey to start my new venture, Maxx Academy. After months of preparation, everything was set—place, infrastructure, syllabus, and most importantly, 20 students had enrolled for the Apparel Merchandising course. We were supposed to start classes on Sunday, and I had planned to secure a faculty member with industry experience to teach the course. Despite all my efforts, I couldn't find the right person.

As the days passed, my anxiety grew. Thursday approached, and the start date loomed large. Panic set in as I faced the reality that I still had no teacher. The students were expecting to begin their journey with us, and I was at a loss. By Thursday night, my stress had reached its peak. I felt utterly lost and helpless. How could I face the students on Sunday without a teacher?

That night, in a state of despair, I turned to prayer. With tears in my eyes, I said, "God, I've done everything I could. I have no other options left. I need a teacher, and I trust you to find one for me." Exhausted and overwhelmed, I went to bed.

In the depths of my sleep, I had a vivid dream. I found myself speaking to a lady named Manpreet. I explained to her the entire concept of the course and the topics we would cover. She listened intently and agreed to work for me as a faculty member. She even mentioned that she had four years of experience. The conversation felt incredibly real, and when I woke up the next morning, her name lingered in my mind .

With renewed hope, I hurried to my office and pulled out my file of resumes. At that time, I was also working as a recruitment consultant, so I had a substantial database of resumes. I called my assistant and asked her to search for a "Manpreet" among the resumes. She looked through the files and, within minutes, found one. Manpreet, with four years of experience, from Faridabad. My assistant, puzzled, asked, "Mam, where do we have to send her?

I smiled, feeling a sense of divine intervention, and replied, "We don't have to send her anywhere. God has sent her to us."

Eagerly, I dialed Manpreet's number, my heart pounding with anticipation. As the phone rang, I couldn't shake the feeling that this was the moment of truth. When she answered, the conversation unfolded just as it had in my dream. It was as if I was reliving the dream in real life. I wanted to meet her before Sunday, so I asked if she was available. She responded, "Mam, you can come during lunch time." When I inquired about her company and address, my heart skipped a beat. It was the same company where I had a meeting with HR scheduled for that day.

The synchronicity was astounding. The universe had indeed conspired to bring us together. That afternoon, I met Manpreet, and we finalized everything. The relief I felt was immeasurable. On Sunday, she stood before the class, ready to teach. Watching her interact with the students, I was filled with an overwhelming sense of gratitude. The tension and stress of the past week melted away, replaced by a profound appreciation for the miraculous way everything had fallen into place.

As Manpreet taught the students, I marvelled at the perfection of it all. I silently thanked God for orchestrating such a perfect solution. Manpreet looked back at me and smiled, a knowing smile that seemed to convey a message from the divine: "Don't ask me how. Just believe."

This experience taught me the magic of believing in the universe's power to provide, even in the darkest of times. The journey from despair to hope to gratitude was a testament to the miraculous ways in which our desires and needs can be met when we trust in something greater than ourselves.

"The Universe is under no obligation to make sense to you."

- Neil De Grasse Tyson

Wish Upon a Board   3

I started my career as a Mind Power Trainer during the COVID-19 pandemic. The world had come to a standstill, and like everyone else, I adapted to the new normal of online sessions. For a whole year, I conducted these virtual sessions, connecting with people through screens. Yet, deep down, I yearned for the energy and connection of a live audience.

One evening, while creating my vision board, I pasted a picture of myself giving a lecture on stage in a packed auditorium. It was a dream, a goal I held close to my heart. Every day, I looked at that board, visualizing myself on that stage, feeling the thrill of addressing a live audience.

But life, as it often does, got busy. My focus shifted to other techniques and sessions, and my vision board ended up in a drawer, forgotten amid the hustle.

Months later, an unexpected opportunity came my way. I was invited to conduct a session at a prestigious college. Excited and nervous, I prepared meticulously, hoping to make a lasting impact.

On the day of the session, I arrived at the college, expecting the usual classroom setup. To my surprise, they led me to the auditorium. My heart raced with anticipation as I walked through the doors. The sight that greeted me was nothing short of magical—a sea of faces, 250 students, filled the hall. The energy was palpable.

As I stood on the stage, it felt like I was reliving a moment from a dream. It was the exact scene from my vision board. The students' eager eyes, the hushed whispers, and the anticipation in the air—it was all just as I had imagined. Even my outfit, a pink sari, matched the one in my vision.

When I began to speak, a wave of emotion swept over me. The words flowed effortlessly, and the audience responded with enthusiasm and applause. It was surreal, almost like an out-of-body experience. The connection I felt with those students was profound, and their engagement fueled my passion.

After the session, I couldn't wait to get home. I rushed to my room, my heart pounding with excitement. Digging through my drawer, I found my vision board. There it was—the picture, the stage, the packed auditorium. Everything was just as I had envisioned.

Tears filled my eyes as I realized the power of my dreams. At that moment, I felt a deep sense of gratitude and awe. It was as if the universe had conspired to make my dream come true. I looked up and asked the universe, "How did this happen? How did I get such a big opportunity exactly like I envisioned?"

And the universe whispered back, "Don't ask me how."

That experience changed me forever. It reaffirmed my belief in the power of visualisation and the importance of holding on to our visions, even when they seem far away. My vision board became a symbol of hope and possibility, a reminder that dreams do come true when we believe in them with all our heart.

Seeing truly is believing.

"Once you make a decision, the Universe conspires to make it happen."

— Ralph Waldo Emerson

From Desperation to Triumph   4

In June 2020, during the first wave of COVID-19, the world felt like it was collapsing. Everything was shut down, including my institute. With no online classes, my income had completely dried up. Every day was a struggle as I desperately searched for a way to make ends meet. I felt lost and hopeless, my dreams and ambitions buried under the weight of uncertainty.

One night, in utter desperation, I surrendered my question to the universe. I asked for guidance, hoping for a miracle. To my surprise, an Idea came to me: start online workshops related to merchandising. It felt like a lifeline in a stormy sea.

Determined to make it work, I threw myself into the project, promoting the workshops on social media with all my energy. Days passed with only three responses. Although they converted into participants, the Income was barely enough to cover basic expenses. The workshop felt like a hollow victory. My heart sank with disappointment.

Feeling defeated, I decided to tap into the power of my mind. I had read about visualization techniques and their ability to manifest reality. With nothing to lose, I started imagining success. I visualized receiving back-to-back payment notifications on my phone. I pictured a screen filled with 50 students, each eager to learn from me. I held onto this vision, repeating it daily, clinging to the hope that things would change.

And then, as if by magic, they did.

One day, a polytechnic in Faridabad reached out, asking me to conduct an online workshop for 50 students. My heart leaped with excitement. I created a vibrant ad and posted it on my

WhatsApp status. Soon after, a university from the south contacted me, followed by another from Noida, each wanting workshops for 40 and 50 students respectively. My dreams were unfolding before my eyes.

I finalized all three workshops and waited for the payments. The anticipation was overwhelming. Then, it happened—my phone started buzzing with payment notifications. One after another, the alerts kept coming. It was exactly as I had visualized. In just 15 days, I went from three students to a staggering 140.

On the first day of training, as I introduced myself and looked at the screen filled with eager faces, I overcame with emotion. "Is this a dream? Is this real? 140 students!" The universe had delivered in ways I couldn't have imagined.

I looked up and silently asked, "How did this happen?" The answer came swiftly, as if whispered by the universe itself, "Don't ask me how."

Tears of gratitude streamed down my face. The journey from desperation to triumph had been nothing short of miraculous. It was a testament to the power of belief, determination, and the mysterious ways of the universe.

That experience reaffirmed my faith in the unseen forces that guide us. It taught me that even in the darkest times, there is always a way forward if we believe in our dreams and stay open to the possibilities.

I believe nothing happens by mistake you know, the Universe has a divine plan. That's sounds dramatic.

- Laul Del Rey

From Wish to Reality

5

In 2019, I started my Fashion Institute, nestled in a cozy residential area. It was a humble beginning, but I had big dreams. One of those dreams was to move my institute to a bustling commercial area, where it could truly thrive. The thought of having a prominent presence in the heart of the market filled me with excitement and determination.

I began searching for a suitable commercial space, visiting different markets and exploring various options. But every place I liked came with a hefty price tag. One particular building caught my eye; it was conveniently close to my home and located right at the center of the market. When I visited the second floor of that building, I knew it was perfect for my needs. However, the landlord's rent demand of ₹ 70,000 was way beyond my budget. Disheartened, I returned home quietly, but the image of that space lingered in my mind. I couldn't shake off the desire to have my institute there.

Every time I passed by that area, I would look at the building and tell myself, "One day, I will have my institute here with the Maxx Academy board right at the top." The vision of that building with my academy's name shining brightly on it became crystal clear in my mind.

A year passed, filled with hope and persistence. Then, one fine day, I received an unexpected call from a fellow educator who ran a coaching academy on the same building's second floor. He had created a beautiful infrastructure but was struggling with the high rent. He proposed sharing the space with me for ₹ 25,000. My heart raced with excitement. This was it! Without hesitation, I agreed, and within a week, I had moved into the fully furnished office with partitions, AC, furniture—everything I needed.

I asked about placing my signboard, and he told me the topmost spot was vacant and I could put my board there. It felt like the universe had whispered "TATHASTU" to my wish. I was now in the same building, on the same floor, with rent within my budget, and the Maxx Academy board right at the top.

The day the laborers fitted the board, I stood there, watching them work with bated breath. When they asked me to check it, I looked up at the board, my heart swelling with gratitude. The sight of Maxx Academy proudly displayed brought tears to my eyes. I looked up at the sky, smiling. This time, I didn't ask any questions. I knew the universe would reply, "Don't ask me how."

This journey from a wish to reality reaffirmed my belief in the power of dreams and the magic of the universe. It taught me that with faith and persistence, even the wildest dreams can come true. My story of Maxx Academy is a testament to the fact that sometimes, you don't need to know how things will happen—just believe that they will.

"There are no extra pieces in the Universe. Everyone is here because he or she has a place to fill, and every piece must fit itself into the big jigsaw puzzle."

- Deepak Chopra

Mastering Manifestation   6

In December 2020, the world was facing a difficult time. The COVID-19 pandemic had turned everything upside down. Schools and colleges were shut down, and learning had become hard. My Institute, which was once full of life, now felt empty and cold. The sound of laughter, students chatting, and the excitement of learning were gone. It broke my heart to see it like this.

I had reopened in October 2020, hoping things would get better, but they didn't. Financial problems were getting worse each day, and I felt like I was drowning. Students couldn't pay their fees, and I couldn't force them because I knew they were struggling too. I felt helpless. Every day, I heard about other institutes closing down, and I feared mine would be next.

By December, everything seemed to be falling apart. No new students were joining, and many were cancelling their enrollments. Bills were piling up—rent, salaries, and other expenses. It felt like a huge weight on my shoulders. I didn't know what to do. I was scared and exhausted. The thought of closing my beloved Institute, the place I had poured my heart and soul into, felt like losing a part of myself. But I saw no other way out.

Then, a memory flashed in my mind. I remembered a workshop I had attended about mind power. It had sounded like magic, almost too good to be true. But I thought, "What if it could help me now?" I decided to give it one last try. I thought of applying all tools and techniques of mind power and believe in myself. I decided to hold on a little longer, even though things looked hopeless.

At first, I was unsure. The months from November to February had always been slow for my

Institute. Especially January—it was always the quietest month. In 13 years, I had never seen any new admissions in January. The idea of trying to survive for another three months seemed impossible. I was tired and scared. But deep down, I knew I had to try. I had no other way to earn money. What did I have to lose?

So, I took a deep breath and decided to give it my all. I began using my mind power training, focusing on what I wanted to achieve. I needed a miracle. I set a goal: I needed at least 10 new students in January 2021 to keep my Institute alive. It felt like a dream, almost impossible. But I threw myself into it with all my heart. Day and night, I blocked out every negative thought and focused on bringing my Institute back to life. I prayed, I believed, and I hoped.

Then, something amazing happened—something I couldn't have imagined. Slowly, things began to change. One by one, new students started joining. I was shocked. January, which was always a quiet month, was suddenly buzzing with new admissions. It felt like a miracle. I couldn't believe my eyes. Each time a new student signed up, my heart filled with joy and relief. The universe was listening to me.

By the end of January 2021, I had managed to pay off the rent and other bills. But that wasn't the best part. I had gained 19 new students—far more than I had ever dreamed of. It was the highest number of new students I had ever seen in one month in the last 12 years I had been running the Institute. Just one month back I was on verge of shutting down my Institute and here I was breaking the record of past 12 years. I was overwhelmed with happiness and gratitude. Just when I had been ready to give up, everything turned around.

On January 31, 2021, I sat at my desk, looking at the numbers on my computer. I typed in "19 new admissions" and stared at the final total. Tears filled my eyes as I smiled. I folded my hands, looked up, and whispered, "I believed you would do it." And a clear answer came back to me, as if from the universe: "Yes, just believe—and don't ask me how".

No, external factors can defeat you if you are strong enough from inside. If you have faith in God, if you trust the universe, you can never be a failure. Situations may come in your life when you find nothing in your favor. But that is the time actually when you need to hold yourself, stay strong, do not let yourself get shattered. Be patient that the favorable time will come. Keep doing efforts and it never goes to waste. Because whatever you are putting in the universe, it has to come back to you. Universe will definitely reward you for your efforts.

"When you bow deeply to the Universe, it bows back, when you call out the name of God, it echoes inside you."

- Morihei Verhiba

A Young Dreamer

7

The story began in my childhood. Though I can't recall the exact age, I must have been between 11 and 16 years old. Those were tough times. My father had passed away by then, leaving a void that my mother tried to fill while shouldering the burden of raising me and my siblings all alone. Since my mother didn't have a job, we relied entirely on my father's pension to get by, which was barely enough to meet our needs. Money was always tight, and luxuries were out of the question.

I developed a strong desire for two things: a wrist watch and a pair of black bellies (shoes). These items were all the rage back then. I first spotted the black bellies in a shop window while walking home from school. They were so beautiful, and I instantly fell in love with them. But I couldn't bring myself to ask my mother to buy them. I knew we couldn't afford such things.

Despite this, my longing for the black bellies and the wrist watch grew stronger each day. Every night before bed, I would close my eyes and imagine myself wearing those black bellies and a shiny new wrist watch. In my dreams, I strutted around proudly, feeling a happiness so intense that it warmed my heart. The sheer pleasure of these dreams made me look forward to bedtime. During the day, whenever I felt sad or hopeless, I would retreat into my imagination, where the black bellies and wrist watch were mine. Those moments of fantasy became my secret sanctuary, a place where everything was perfect.

One ordinary day, my elder sister came to visit us. She was married and often came over to help my mother and look after us. That day, she arrived with a mysterious packet in her hand. She called me over and, with a playful smile, asked me to guess what was inside. I guessed it might be a dress or a doll, something she would usually bring.

With growing curiosity, I took the packet from her and carefully opened it. My heart raced as I lifted the lid of the box. To my astonishment, inside were the exact black bellies I had been dreaming about! I was overwhelmed with joy and couldn't believe my eyes. But the surprises didn't end there. My sister then asked me to give her my hand. She gently slipped a watch onto my wrist—a beautiful digital watch with a black dial and a mustard-coloured strap.

At that moment, my dream had come true. The black bellies and the wrist watch were real, and they were mine. I was filled with a mix of disbelief and pure happiness. As I wore my new black bellies and the wrist watch, I felt an immense sense of gratitude and awe. It wasn't just about having the things I had wanted so badly; It was about realizing that dreams and desires have a power of their own.

I looked at my sister, tears of joy welling up in my eyes, and asked her, "Didi, how did you know I wanted these? I never told anyone."

She just smiled and kissed my forehead. Her smile was warm and knowing, as if she had tapped into some mysterious force. She kept on smiling as if saying "Don't ask me How?"

That was the first time I truly felt the power of the universe. It was as if my deep desire and vivid imagination had sent out a message to the cosmos, and my sister had received it.

The universe listens to our deepest wishes in ways we cannot always understand. Because sometimes, the magic of the universe works in mysterious ways, and all we need to do is believe in the power of our dreams.

"If you want to find the secrets of the Universe, think in terms of energy, frequency and vibrations."

– Nikola Tesla

The Universe's Canvas

8

On a warm morning in September 2023, I received an invitation to attend a workshop organized by a group known for their amazing training programs. As I walked into the building, a strange feeling of familiarity swept over me. It was like stepping into a dream that I had forgotten, but now suddenly remembered. I realized, with a burst of excitement, that this was the place I had always wanted to be—a place where I longed to learn, grow, and, deep down, teach.

The session started, and I sat down among the 35 other people in the room. Everything felt just right—the lights, the seats, the energy in the room. But as I sat there, my mind began to wander. A small, quiet wish popped up in my head. What if one day, I'm not sitting here as a participant, but standing up there as the professional trainer? I could almost see it—me holding a microphone, changing the slides, and talking to a room full of eager learners. The picture in my head was so clear, it felt like I was living it right then and there. My heart filled with a mix of excitement and hope, making my pulse race and my breath catch.

For the next two hours, while the session went on, I was only half paying attention. The other half of me was lost in the movie playing in my mind. It felt so real, so close, that I couldn't help but smile. But when the session ended, I let go of the dream, sending it out into the universe with a simple request: Make it happen. Then, I got busy with my life—training sessions at schools, colleges, and other places. The dream, once so clear, slowly faded as my days became full of work.

Months went by, and suddenly, it was March 2024. One day, my phone rang out of the blue. It was a call from the same organization where I had attended that workshop. My heart skipped a beat as they asked If I would like to lead a training session for industry professionals. The topic was soft skills, something I loved to teach. I agreed, not knowing that the universe had already started to work its magic.

The day of the session came, and as I got ready to leave, I received another call from the session organizer. Curious, I asked how many people were expected. Her answer caught me by surprise: "Only 4-5 people. It's just a test session to see how it goes." A wave of disappointment hit me. I had imagined a room full of eager learners, not just a few. But before I let the sadness take over, I decided to take a moment for myself. I sat down, closed my eyes, and once again imagined a room full of 30 people, all excited and ready to learn. I let that happy feeling fill me up before heading out the venue.

As I entered the conference room, I noticed that it was crowded with participants, with some additional chairs being arranged for seating. I was astonished and inquired. According to the coordinator, there was a last-minute plan change and we have extended the invitation to more participants. There were 32 participants in total. I was filled with happiness and enthusiasm.

The session went by quickly, full of slides, talks, and activities. When it was over, I went home feeling satisfied but tired. It wasn't until later, when the organization sent me the photos from the session, that something amazing hit me.

As I looked through the pictures, one image made me stop. There I was, standing at the front of the podium, holding the microphone, with the slides changing behind me on the screen. I came to the realization that this place was my intended destination as a trainer, not as a participant. I accomplished the same thing here today. The room, the podium, the way I was talking to the participants—it was exactly how I had imagined it. My heart swelled with emotions as I realized what had happened. The universe had remembered my wish, even when I had let it slip from my mind.

In that moment, it felt like my dream and reality had become one, creating a moment so perfect, so right, that it gave me chills. A warm smile spread across my face as I whispered, "How did you remember?" And almost immediately, a quiet voice from within answered, "Don't ask me how".

At times, we do not get the results we expected for but even in that situation we should be grateful for what we have received. It does not mean you become complacent with whatever you have. There is always a scope of improvement in ours. Whatever the result has come, accept what you have received, learn and move ahead to make more improvements next time.

When we are thankful to the universe, acknowledge what it has given us, then you will attract more of what you wish for, but if we complain of not having it, according to our expectations, then chances are of receiving less next time. So be grateful for whatever universe gives you.

"The Universe whispered in my ear- Continue to share your heart and I promise when the time is right, I will deliver you the most amazing love. Just believe."

- Albert Einstein

Finding Purpose Beyond Success

9

If you truly love something from the core of your heart, the universe conspires to bring it to you, as long as your intention is pure.

For years, I ran my fashion institute. Since 2009, I had built a name in the industry. My students respected me, and from the outside, it seemed like I had everything—a successful business, a steady reputation, and the admiration of many. Yet, deep down, something was missing. I felt a strange emptiness, a hollow space inside me that no amount of external success could fill.

Every night, as I lay in bed, a thought would tug at me—*Is this really it? Is this what I'm meant to do for the rest of my life?* The dissatisfaction grew louder, and I couldn't shake the feeling that there was something more, something bigger out there for me. I couldn't understand why, despite all I had achieved, I wasn't satisfied. It wasn't that I didn't love my work, but there was a part of me yearning for something deeper, more meaningful.

It was then that I started probing the question that haunted me: *What is my purpose?* I didn't even know what a life purpose was supposed to look like. But slowly, as I reflected, the answer began to emerge. It wasn't fashion that truly moved me—it was connecting with people, guiding them, especially women who needed support. I realized that counseling was where my heart truly lay. The joy I felt when I helped others, when I listened to their stories and offered guidance, was unlike anything else.

I felt a fire within me, a burning desire to empower underprivileged women, to give them the skills and knowledge they needed to change their lives. But I was lost—*How do I start? Where do I begin?* The uncertainty overwhelmed me, but I didn't let it stop me. I made a firm decision and surrendered my dream to the universe. I asked it to bring me into alignment with my purpose.

Every day, I began visualizing. I would close my eyes and see myself standing in front of a group of 50-60 women from humble backgrounds, teaching them, guiding them, helping them find their strength. I saw myself teaching them stitching, helping them build a future. It became a ritual, my daily prayer to the universe.

And then, as if by magic, things started to shift. One day, out of the blue, an industrialist approached me. He told me about an NGO he was starting, aimed at empowering women. They needed someone to manage the administration and lead the initiative, to teach both technical and soft skills. My heart skipped a beat. *Could this be it?* I could hardly believe my ears.

Without hesitation, I said yes. Within 15 days, everything was ready—the space, the infrastructure, and the first batch of women. And then the day arrived, the day that would change my life forever. I stood in front of 62 women, their eyes filled with hope and curiosity, just as I had imagined. As I began to speak, I felt a deep sense of gratitude wash over me. This was exactly what I had visualized—down to the smallest detail.

At that moment, I knew that I was on the right path. The universe had conspired to bring me here, to this very moment. Today, I continue to work with that NGO, helping women find their own strength and purpose. Many of them have gone on to build successful lives, and every time I see one of them succeed, I am reminded of the power of intention and faith.

Sometimes, I still wonder how it all happened so quickly, how everything fell into place in just 15 days. But the universe whispers back to me, "Don't ask me how."

"You are the one who calls the law of attraction into action, and you do it through your thoughts."

- Rhonde Byrne

Dream, Believe, Achieve

10

In 2020, as my daughter was nearing the end of high school, she had her heart set on one particular college. It was her dream to study there, and I wanted to support her in every way possible. I introduced her to the idea of visualization and vision board—two powerful tools that can help turn dreams into reality. We spent time exploring different techniques to harness the mind's potential, and she embraced them with enthusiasm.

One of the key practices we focused on was creating a vision board. She filled it with images of her dream college—pictures of the campus, the classrooms, and even the college's logo. She then made this vision board her phone and tablet wallpaper, so she could see it every day. These daily visual reminders helped her keep her goal in sight, motivating her to work towards it with determination.

But visualization alone wasn't enough; she knew she had to put in the effort. So, alongside her positive mindset, she studied diligently, keeping her focus on the goal. She believed in herself, trusting that all the hard work, combined with her positive thinking, would lead to success.

I'm incredibly proud to say that her dedication and belief in herself paid off. Not only did she get accepted into her dream college, but she also received an impressive scholarship, which was a testament to both her hard work and her positive mindset.

Watching her journey was truly inspiring. It showed me the power of visualization, determination, and the belief that with the right mindset and effort, dreams can indeed become reality.

"I have a naive trust in the universe that at some level it all makes sense, and we can get glimpses of that sense if we try."

-Mihaly Csikszentmihalyi

Are you eager to understand the "how" behind these stories? In the upcoming chapters, I'll guide you on how to practice and experience miracles in your own life. By following the Universe's algorithms, you'll discover that miracles aren't just possible—they're inevitable.

Chapter 1
Clarity: The Key to Getting What You Want

Many times, we don't even know exactly what we want. We might have a vague idea, but it's not clear. However, the universe works on the principle of clarity. The clearer you are about what you want, the more likely you are to receive it. So, it's important to be clear about what you want.

For example, if you say, "I want a good job with a good salary," that's not clear enough. Your subconscious mind doesn't know what "good" means, and neither does the universe. The words "good" and "bad" are just labels, and they can mean different things to different people. To get what you really want, you have to be specific.

Start by defining what "good" means to you. Is a good salary ₹ 50,000 per month? Or maybe ₹ 10,000 per month? What kind of job would be a good job for you? What should your job title be? What kind of work do you want to do? The universe needs clarity and detail. The more detailed and specific you are, the better the universe can help you.

Here's how you can gain clarity:

1. Define What You Want

First, take some time to think about what you really want. Be as specific as possible. If you want a good job, describe exactly what that job looks like. What company would you like to work for? What would your job title be? How much would you like to earn? Write down all the details. The clearer you are, the better.

2. Set a Clear Intention

Once you've defined what you want, the next step is to set a clear intention. This means you focus your mind on your goal and tell the universe exactly what you want. Your intention should be specific, not vague. For example, instead of saying, "I want a good job," say, "I want a job as a software developer at XYZ company with a salary of $50,000 a year."

3. Don't Limit Yourself

When you set your intention, don't limit yourself. Sometimes we think that achieving our goals depends only on what we can do. But when you surrender your goals to the universe, it's not just you who is working on them. The universe, with its unlimited power, starts working for you. Remember, there are no limitations in the universe. Anything is possible. So don't set small goals because you think you're not capable of more. Dream big, and trust that the universe will help you.

Clarity is the first and most important step in achieving your goals. The more clear and detailed you are about what you want, the more the universe can help you. So, take the time to define your goals clearly, set a strong intention, and then trust the universe to work its magic. Remember, there are no limits in the universe, so don't limit yourself. The universe is always ready to help you, but it needs you to be clear about what you want.

Chapter 2

The Power of Focus: Nurturing Your Goals

Imagine you're standing at the starting line of a race. You know where the finish line is, and you're excited to get there. But here's the secret: It's not just about running fast; it's about staying focused on that finish line until you reach it. In life, the goals you set are like that finish line, and your focus is what will help you get there.

You've probably heard the saying, "Energy flows wherever the focus goes." This means that whatever you put your focus on will grow stronger. Think of it like a plant. If you don't water a plant, it will eventually wilt and die. But if you give it the care and attention it needs, it will grow into something beautiful. Your goals work the same way—they need your focus and energy to grow into something great.

When you set a goal, it's like planting a seed. But just planting the seed isn't enough. You have to nurture it, pay attention to it, and keep working on it. Every time you think about your goal, every action you take toward it, you're giving it the energy it needs to grow.

Staying focused isn't always easy, though. There are distractions everywhere—things that can pull your attention away from what you really want. But if you remind yourself every day of what you're working toward, you can stay on track. Imagine your goal as a shining star in the sky. Even if clouds cover it for a while, you know it's still there. You just need to keep moving in its direction.

Every day, take time to think about your goal. What do you want to achieve? What steps can you take today to get closer to it? Even small steps are important because they add up over time. When you keep your goal in mind, you're giving it the energy it needs to grow. And as you stay focused, you'll find that you start to make real progress.

Your mind Is a powerful tool. Keeping it positive and focused on your goal is like giving it the fuel it needs to keep going. If you start to feel discouraged, remind yourself of why you set this goal in the first place. Believe that you can achieve it. A positive mindset Is like sunshine for your dreams—it helps them grow stronger and brighter.

Practicing mindfulness can also help you stay focused. Mindfulness means paying attention to what you're doing right now, without getting distracted by other thoughts. It's about being fully present in the moment. When you practice mindfulness, it's easier to focus on your goals because your mind is clear and calm.

Another important factor in staying focused is getting enough sleep. Sleep is like a reset button for your brain. When you get a good night's sleep, your mind is refreshed and ready to take on the day. You'll find it much easier to concentrate and stay focused when you're well-rested. On the other hand, if you're tired, it's harder to stay on track, and you might lose some of the energy you need to keep moving forward.

Here's a helpful tip: Every morning, take a moment to remind yourself of your goal. Ask yourself, "What do I want to achieve today?" Starting your day with this thought will help you stay focused throughout the day. And before you go to bed, think about your goal again. Remind yourself of why it's important to you. These are two powerful moments—when you wake up and when you're about to sleep—because that's when your subconscious mind is most active. Focusing on your goals during these times can help you achieve them faster because your mind will keep working on them, even while you sleep.

In the end, staying focused is about giving consistent energy to your goals. It's like watering your dreams every day, making sure they grow strong and healthy. The more you stay focused, the closer you'll get to reaching your dreams. So, take it one step at a time, keep your eyes on the finish line, and watch how your focus can turn your dreams into reality.

Chapter 3

Energy of Emotions: How to Raise Your Vibrations

Everything in this universe is vibrating at a certain frequency, including us. This means that we are like magnets, constantly attracting things that match our own vibrations. According to the Law of Attraction, "like attracts like." In simple words, whatever our vibrations are, we are going to attract similar things into our lives.

But what are these vibrations, and where do they come from? Our vibrations depend on how we feel—our emotions. Think about your emotions throughout the day. Are you feeling happy, grateful, or peaceful? If so, you're vibrating at a high frequency, and you will attract more of those good things into your life. On the other hand, if you're feeling sad, angry, or fearful, those are lower vibrations, and you might attract things that match those feelings.

High vibrations come from positive emotions like love, compassion, gratitude, joy, happiness, and peace. So, if you want good things to happen in your life, it's important to keep your emotions in that high-vibration zone. But what about lower vibrations? These come from emotions like fear, guilt, shame, anger, hatred, grief, and sadness. If you're stuck in these lower emotions, your vibrations drop, and it's like sending out signals to attract more negative things. That's why it's so Important to release these negative emotions and let go of them.

The truth is that the universe doesn't give you what you want; it gives you what you are. This means that the kind of emotions you have and the vibrations you send out are what you will attract back into your life. So, it's really important to keep a check on your emotions. Stay positive, keep your vibrations high, and you will attract positivity.

Now, how do we raise our vibrations? Here are some simple ways:

1. **Gratitude** – Gratitude is one of the easiest and most powerful ways to raise your vibration. Being thankful for what you have in your life instantly lifts your emotions. Start by counting your blessings. Be thankful for your life, your body, your eyes, your hands, and your heart. You can also be thankful for your family, friends, education, and even the money you have. Don't forget to be thankful for nature—the air you breathe, the water you drink, and the sunlight that warms you. When you focus on your blessings, you will attract more blessings into your life. Start each day with gratitude, and watch how your vibrations soar!

2. **Connect with Nature** – Spending time in nature can be very calming and refreshing.

When you're in nature, you can let go of the lower vibrations and replace them with the calming and vibrant energy of the natural world. Whether it's a walk in the park, sitting by a tree, or listening to the birds, nature helps to raise your vibrations.

3. **Exercise Regularly and Eat a Healthy Diet –** Moving your body is another great way to raise your vibrations. Exercise, like yoga, walking, or going to the gym, helps release any stuck or stagnant energy in your body. And don't forget about food! High-vibration foods like fresh fruits and vegetables carry life energy from the Earth and the sun. Eating these healthy foods helps to keep your body and mind at a high vibrational state.

4. **Meditate–** Meditation is a wonderful way to reduce stress and anxiety. When you meditate, you quiet your mind, and this helps you stay calm and focused throughout

the day. Meditation also keeps your vibrations high by helping you stay mindful and connected to the present moment.

5. **Surround Yourself with Positive People –** The people you spend time with can affect your emotions and vibrations. That's why it's important to surround yourself with people who have a positive mindset. If you're around people who are always negative, their energy can bring your vibrations down. So, choose to be with people who lift you up and make you feel good.

By working on raising your vibrations, you're taking another important step toward your goals. When you focus on your goals, take daily actions, and keep your vibrations high, you are aligning yourself with what you want to attract into your life. So, keep your vibrations high, stay positive, and watch how the universe responds by sending good things your way!

Chapter 4

Taking Action: Turning Your Plans into Reality

Once you have a clear picture of your goal and have done the planning, the next step is taking action. A plan, no matter how perfect it looks on paper, will remain just that—a plan—if you don't take action. Action is what creates momentum and keeps you focused and motivated to achieve your goals.

Write It Down

Start by writing down your action plan. Make a checklist of the tasks you need to complete and the resources you'll need to reach your goal. Writing things down can help declutter your mind and make your path clearer. When everything is on paper, you can see exactly what you need to do and when. This clarity makes it easier to take the next step.

Once you've written everything down, it's time to prepare yourself to start taking action. Here are some key points to remember:

1. No Excuses

When it comes to taking action, there should be no room for excuses. You need to develop a mindset of a go-getter—someone who doesn't let anything stand in their way. Our mind is very powerful. If you are determined to do something, your mind will give you ideas and solutions to help you move forward. But if you start thinking you can't do it, your mind will give you excuses instead. So, always tune your mind toward action. Remind yourself that no matter how hard it seems, you can do it.

2. There Is No Perfect Moment

Sometimes we wait for the perfect moment to act, thinking that things will get easier or that the timing will be just right. But the truth is, there's no such thing as a perfect moment. If you keep waiting for the "right time," you may never take action. The perfect moment is now. Don't delay your progress by waiting for the stars to align.

Start now, with what you have, and trust that everything will fall into place as you move forward.

3. Taking the First Step

The journey of success is made up of many steps, but it all begins with one important step—the first one. This first step can feel difficult or scary, and you might feel resistance. But taking that first step is crucial. It's the push that gets you started. Once you take it, you'll find that the next steps come more easily. Your journey begins the moment you decide to act, so don't wait—take that first step today.

4. Accept Failure

Failure is not the opposite of success; it's a part of it. On your journey, you will make mistakes and experience setbacks. But failure is just a stepping stone to success. Don't be afraid of it. Instead, accept it as part of the process. When you face failure, learn from it, adjust your course, and keep moving forward. Every successful person has faced failure at some point, but what sets them apart is their determination to keep going despite the setbacks.

5. Keep Moving Forward

Taking action is the key to turning your dreams into reality. It's what moves you from the planning stage to actually achieving your goals. With the right mindset—no excuses, no waiting for the perfect moment, and a willingness to accept failure—you can achieve anything you set your mind to.

Remember, the journey to success begins with that first step. Don't wait. Start taking action today, and watch how your efforts turn your plans into reality.

Chapter 5

The Power of Visualization

Everything we create begins with a thought. First, it appears in our mind, and then it becomes real in the world. Imagine this: every invention you know, like the light bulb, airplane, or even the gramophone, started as an idea in someone's mind. The scientist or inventor saw it in their imagination before they brought it into reality. This shows us how powerful our thoughts and imagination are.

Now, it's your turn! If you want to achieve something, the first step is to visualize it. But what does that mean? Visualization is like creating a mental picture of what you want. You imagine the final result, as if you've already achieved your goal.

Let's say your goal is to own your dream house. Start by picturing it in your mind. See the house from the outside first. What color is it? Does it have a garden? Imagine a nameplate with your name on it. Then, walk inside in your mind. Visualize you" living room. What does the furniture look like? What color are the walls? Do you have paintings or pictures hanging up?

As you imagine yourself in your dream house, think about how happy you would feel living there with your family. Picture yourself enjoying each room. Maybe you have a study where you sit and read your favorite books or work on your school projects. Imagine yourself spending an entire day in your house, from morning until night.

But here's the most important part: while you are visualizing, you need to feel the emotions. How would it feel to actually live in that house? Would you be happy? Excited? Peaceful? These emotions are like magical energy. They send out vibrations into the universe, and these vibrations help to attract the things you want into your life.

So, when you visualize, make sure to feel good about it. Let yourself experience the joy of having your dream house as if it's already yours. After you finish visualizing, don't forget to say thank you. Gratitude is a way of showing that you believe your wish has already been fulfilled. It's like saying, "Thank you, Universe, for making my dream come true!"

Visualization is a powerful tool that can help you turn your dreams into reality. By creating clear pictures in your mind and feeling positive emotions, you can attract the life you desire. So, start practicing visualization today and watch how your thoughts become real!

Chapter 6

Trusting the Flow: The Power of Surrender

Surrendering is like releasing a tight grip on something you're holding and allowing it to flow freely. Instead of trying to control every detail of your life, surrendering means trusting that the universe will guide you and work alongside you to make your wishes come true. Imagine trying to hold onto a balloon with all your strength. The harder you try to grip it, the more it resists and struggles to escape. But when you gently let go, the balloon can float freely and reach its destination. This is similar to what happens when you surrender.

As human beings, we have limitations. We can only do so much on our own, and we can't always see the bigger picture. The universe, however, is limitless. It has no boundaries and can create infinite possibilities. When you surrender to the universe, you are placing your trust in this greater, boundless power. You are acknowledging that there are forces beyond your control that can help you achieve your goals in ways you might not have imagined.

Surrendering means letting go of the need to control every aspect of your life. It's about accepting that you can't always manage every situation or outcome. Instead of fighting against the flow of events or struggling with your circumstances, you choose to be open to whatever comes your way. This doesn't mean giving up on your dreams or goals. It means trusting that things will work out in the best possible way, even if it's different from what you expected.

When you practice surrender, you start to notice how things begin to align in surprising ways. You might find that people you need to meet come into your life, new ideas pop into your mind, and circumstances change in your favor. This is the universe working to connect the dots and bring your desires to life. You begin to see synchronicity—the meaningful coincidences that show you that everything is falling into place as it should.

Surrendering also involves letting go of your worries and anxieties. Instead of holding onto fears about what might go wrong, you give these worries to the universe. This act of letting go helps you find a sense of peace. You start to believe that everything is happening for a reason, and that reason is for your greater good. When you're at peace and not resisting, the energy around you flows more smoothly. This allows you to receive what you need with greater ease.

One of the key aspects of surrendering is being open to the possibility that the results you seek might come from unexpected sources. Sometimes, the things you need or the answers you're looking for don't come in the way you planned. They might come from people, places, or situations you hadn't considered. By being open to these surprises, you allow the universe to deliver what you need in the most effective way.

In summary, surrendering is about letting go of the need to control every detail and trusting in a higher power or the universe to guide you. It's about being open to receiving help and support in unexpected ways. When you surrender, you let go of stress and resistance, allowing your energy to flow freely and attract positive outcomes. This openness and trust help you move closer to your goals and dreams, often in ways that are more beautiful and fulfilling than you could have imagined.

Chapter -7

Believe In Divine Timing

Once you've formulated your wish, it's likely that you'll be asked to tap into your subconscious mind. While working on raising your vibration, it's crucial to believe in the universe's ability to fulfill your desires. Trust the universe completely, leaving no room for doubt, fear, or anxiety. Everything has its own perfect timing, and your wish will be granted when you're ready to receive it vibrationally.

Believing means trusting in something, even when you can't see it happening yet. It's like planting a seed in the ground. You can't see the plant right away, but you believe that with water, sunlight, and time, it will grow.

As humans, we have limits to what we can do. We can't control everything around us, and sometimes, no matter how hard we try, things don't go the way we planned. This can make us feel sad, angry, or even scared. But here's something amazing—there is a power in the universe that has no limits. This power can guide us and help us, even when things seem impossible.

When you believe, you are trusting this higher power to work with you. You don't need to worry about how everything will happen; you just need to have faith that it will. When you believe, you stop fighting with your problems. Instead, you open your heart to whatever comes your way.

Believing is also about letting go of fear. When you believe, you let go of trying to control everything and instead allow the universe to do its magic. This doesn't mean you stop working hard or that you don't care. It means you trust that there is a bigger plan at work and that the universe is always working to bring good things into your life.

When you truly believe, you will start to notice that things begin to fall into place. People, ideas, and opportunities will show up, almost as if by magic, to help you reach your dreams. This is called synchronicity, and it's a sign that you are in the flow of the universe.

Believing is not just about thinking positively; it's about feeling calm and trusting that everything will work out. When you believe, you let go of your worries, and you find peace inside yourself. This peaceful feeling helps you stay open to receiving the good things the universe is bringing to you.

Sometimes, what you believe will happen comes from an unexpected place. Maybe you were hoping for help from a friend, but instead, you find help from a stranger. Believing means being open to all the different ways that your wish can come true.

So, believe with all your heart. Trust that the universe has a plan for you, and that plan is for your greater good. When you believe, you create space for miracles to happen in your life. And those miracles can come from anywhere, at any time. All you need to do is believe.

Chapter 8

Affirmations: Your Personal Mantra

Affirmations are like special words that help you feel better and make positive changes in your life. They are positive phrases that you repeat to yourself to boost your mood and challenge any negative thoughts you might have.

When you visualize your goals, it's a great idea to add affirmations to your routine. After you finish imagining your dreams, say these affirmations to yourself. They help you believe in yourself and improve your mood.

Here are some examples of affirmations you can use:

1. Today is the best day of my life.
2. I believe in myself.

3. I accept myself as I am.
4. I am limitless. Anything is possible.
5. I am worthy of love.

How you can Make Your Own Affirmations:

Start with "I am": Begin your affirmation with "I am" and write something positive about yourself. For example, "I am smart."

1. Be Realistic: Make sure your affirmations are achievable and true for you.

2. Keep Them Short: Short and simple affirmations are easier to remember and repeat.

3. Repeat Daily: Say your affirmations every morning when you wake up and every night before you go to bed. You can say them out loud 5 to 10 times.

4. Avoid Negatives: Focus on what you want, not what you don't want. Instead of saying, "I don't fail," say, "I am successful."

5. Use Present Tense: Talk about yourself in the present. For example, say "I am healthy" instead of "I am healing."

Here are some positive affirmations to get you started:

1. I am confident and I am enough.
2. I find joy in everything I do.
3. My body is healthy and my mind is peaceful.
4. I am safe and I am strong.
5. I am ready and capable to handle everything.
6. I see the positive in every situation.
7. I am loved and supported by the universe.
8. I am worthy of love and happiness.

9. I am enough.
10. I see my goals clearly.
11. I am a priority.
12. I believe in myself.
13. All my feelings are valid.
14. I am divinely guided and supported by the universe.
15. Everything I need is within me.
16. I express myself freely.
17. I design my own life.
18. I greet each day with gratitude, hope, and positivity.
19. I get better and better every single day.
20. I am resilient, strong, and brave.

Using affirmations is like giving yourself a boost of confidence and positivity. By repeating these positive phrases, you help your mind focus on what's good and right in your life. So, start using affirmations today and watch how they can make a difference in how you feel and what you achieve!

Chapter 9

Embrace the Joy of Success

When you ask the universe for something and it gives you what you wished for, that's a moment to celebrate! Imagine that the universe has listened to your desires and made your dreams come true. Now, it's your turn to show your gratitude and joy. Saying "thank you" to the universe is an important way to recognize that your wish has been fulfilled.

Celebrating your success, no matter how small, is more than just a way to feel good. It sends a powerful message to the universe that you appreciate what you've received. Whether it's achieving a big goal or just a small step in the right direction, take the time to celebrate it. Smile, be happy, and feel grateful for what the universe has given you. This is a way of honoring the gifts and opportunities you've received.

Think about how you feel when you give someone a gift. If that person shows happiness and gratitude, it makes you feel good, right? You'd probably want to give them something again because their joy makes your effort feel worthwhile. But if the person doesn't seem to care or doesn't say thank you, you might not feel like giving them another gift..

It's the same with the universe. When you celebrate your success and show gratitude, it's like telling the universe, "I'm so thankful for what you've given me." The universe responds to that positive energy and is more likely to bring you even more good things in the future. On the other hand, if you don't celebrate or show appreciation, it's like telling the universe that you didn't notice or didn't care. And just like with the gift example, the universe may not feel as eager to send you more blessings.

Let's think about some small successes you might experience. Maybe you did well on a school project, made a new friend, or helped someone out. These may seem like little things, but they're still achievements. Celebrate them! Maybe you didn't reach your big goal yet, but every step toward it is a success. Celebrate that progress, too.

How do you celebrate? It doesn't have to be anything fancy. You can simply take a moment to smile, say "thank you" to the universe, and feel proud of yourself. You might want to write down what you've achieved and how it makes you feel. Or you could share your happiness with a friend or family member. The key is to acknowledge that you've done something good and to feel joy about it.

Gratitude is a powerful feeling. It opens up your heart and makes you more aware of all the good things in your life. When you celebrate and feel grateful, you raise your vibration. This higher vibration attracts more positive experiences and opportunities into your life. It's like a cycle: the more you celebrate and give thanks, the more the universe gives you reasons to celebrate.

So, always remember to celebrate your successes, both big and small. Say "thank you" to the universe, feel grateful, and get ready to receive even more wonderful things in your life. Celebrating your success is a way of telling the universe that you're ready for even more blessings to come your way!

Chapter 10

Pursuing your Passion

Every person is born with a unique purpose. However, most of us go through life without recognizing this purpose. God has created each of us in a special way, giving us a unique talent. Sometimes, we are aware of this talent, but other times, we may not even know it exists. Our purpose in life is closely tied to this hidden talent. It is our job to discover it.

Once you identify your talent and your purpose in life, you will notice that everything around you starts to align. This happens because the universe begins to help you achieve your desires and goals. You were made specifically for this purpose, and now that you have found it, the universe will support you. This is called alignment with the divine or alignment with the universe.

When you are aligned with your purpose, there is no longer any resistance. Everything will flow smoothly. You might even start to witness some miracles. The universe will surprise you with its gifts, signaling that you are on the right path and fulfilling the purpose you were created for.

To find your purpose, ask yourself what gives you fulfillment and satisfaction. Make time to pursue it. One significant benefit of doing what you love is that it raises your vibrations. High vibrations attract more positive experiences into your life. Keep your vibrations high by recognizing your purpose and doing what you truly enjoy from the heart.

In conclusion, Understanding your purpose in life is crucial. It brings you into alignment with the universe, allowing everything to flow effortlessly.

By pursuing what you love, you not only find fulfillment but also attract more positivity and miracles into your life.

"God or the Universe never hurries and his plans are unknown to us, are never rushed."

- Carol Crandel

My Gratitude Journal

THANK YOU!

- Thank you to the supreme being for the miracles that have strengthened my belief.
- Thank you to my mother who passed on the virtue of being strong to me, the virtue of unwavering faith in God, and for making me independent.
- Thank you to my father, who was not physically present but always an inspiration for being a good human being.
- Thank you to my brother, Mr. Alok Chaudhary, and sister-in-law. They have always supported me like my backbone. He never let me feel the absence of my father. Not much older than me, but he fulfilled all his responsibilities towards me.
- Thank you to my sisters for all the love and care as their younger sibling. Special thanks to my brother-in-law, Dr. Devendra

Chaudhary, for always being a father figure and supporting me.
- Thank you to my daughters, Himika and Diksha, who are my world. Experiencing motherhood through them is the best feeling.
- Thank you to my mentor, Mr. Prateek Pathak, who guided and supported me in my most difficult phase, believed in me, and honored me by giving me an opportunity to join him as a team member.
- Thank you to my guide, who has been like my elder sister, Ms. Meenu Raman, for always being there for me.
- Thank you to my student, Sita, who has always played the role of my friend, mother, sister, and well-wisher.
- Thank you to my best friend and soul sister, Ruchi, who has been consistently present in the highs and lows of my life.
- Thank you to all my students for giving me so much love, respect, and regard.
- Thank you to my office staff and team for believing in me, working towards my goals, and supporting me always.

- I want to thank my young and bright editor, Ms. Divya Pherwani, for bringing out this book.
- Thank you, readers, for reading my book.
- This is my way of showing gratitude. You can also write your gratitude journal for things, miracles, or loved ones you are grateful for.

Your Gratitude Journal

www.ingramcontent.com/pod-product-compliance
Lightning Source LLC
LaVergne TN
LVHW041533070526
838199LV00046B/1655